# James Dean

## a portrait

Roy Schatt

*Delilah*

Distributed by G. P. Putnam's Sons
New York

To Elaine Vorgetts . . .
. . . my playmate for twenty-two years, who typed my longhand
and edited it many times, whose legwork brought together the
necessary people and things, and whose constant concern for
my mental and physical well-being made this book possible.

Published by Delilah Books
A Division of Delilah Communications Ltd.
118 East 25th Street
New York, N.Y. 10010

Library of Congress Catalog Card Number: LC 81-71009

ISBN: 0-933328-24-9

Manufactured in the United States of America

THIS IS A RUGGLES DE LATOUR, INC., BOOK • NEW YORK

*Cover: The most famous of the "Torn Sweater" pictures of James Dean, reproduced world-wide. Frontispiece p. 1: Self
portrait of James Dean and author Roy Schatt. Frontispiece p. 2: Roy Schatt caught James Dean walking towards
him, the wind blowing his clothes against him, his attention elsewhere. This is the second most reproduced picture of
the Schatt/Dean photographs.*

# Contents

# "Torn Sweater" Series

The following group of photos is known as the Torn Sweater Series. The second shot has become perhaps the best known picture of Dean. It was used as a backdrop for the stage revue, *Grease,* on six- and twelve-sheets outside of theaters, and sold as posters worldwide.

I shot the series on December 29, 1954, at the request of *Life* Magazine. They never ran in *Life,* but it didn't seem to affect their popularity.

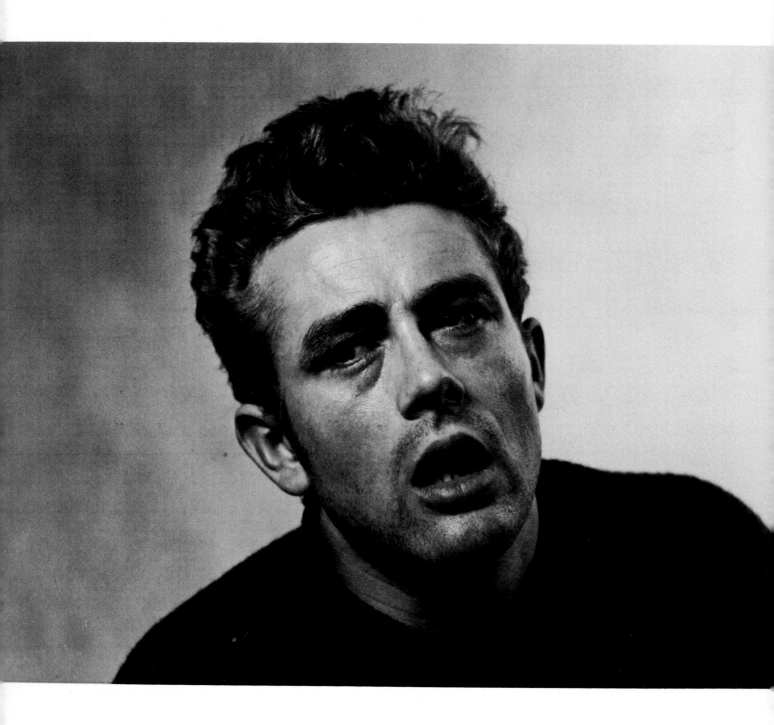

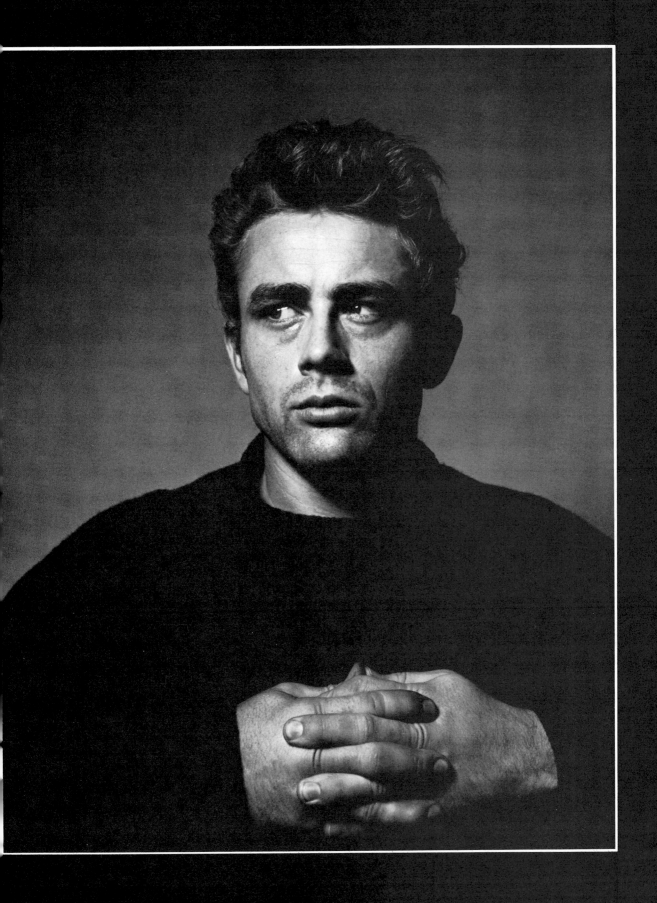

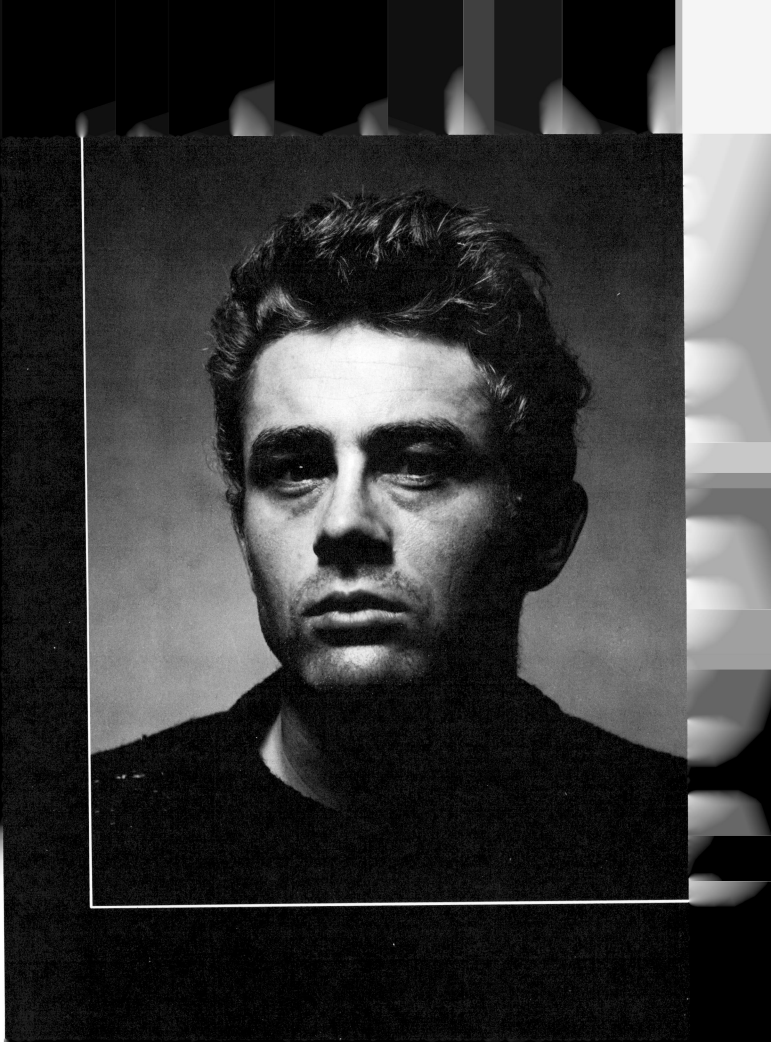

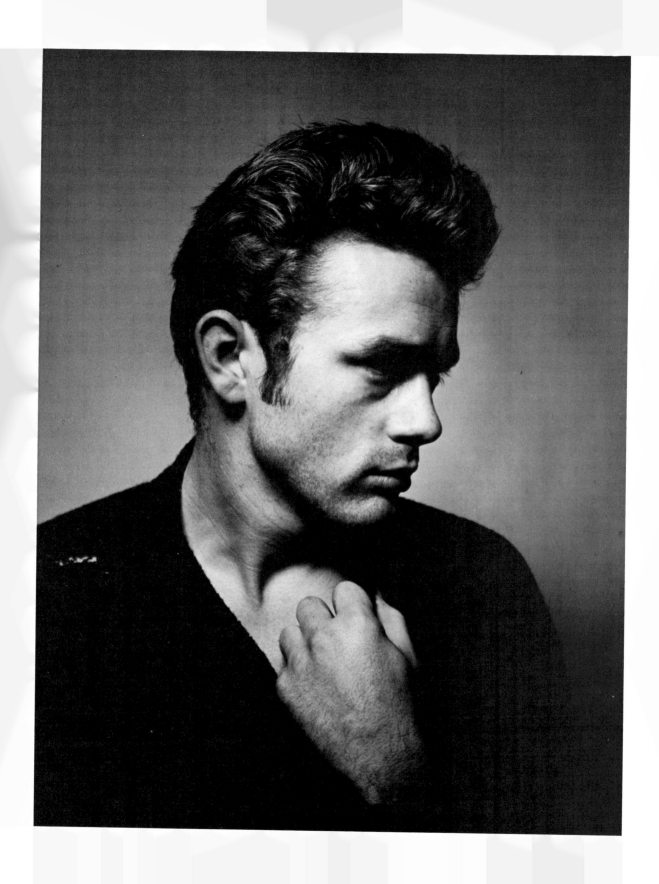

# Remembering James Dean

I knew James Dean from February 1954 until he died in September 1955. I knew him as a friend and as a student. He was a disrupter of norms, a bender of rules, a disquieter of calm. Through the following pictures and vignettes, I hope to transmit a glimpse of his most insistent, and perhaps eternal, presence.

When James Dean asked me to teach him photography I felt much as I did later when Elia Kazan (who directed Dean in *East of Eden*) asked me to teach *him* photography: "You?" I said to Kazan. "Me teach you? Give me one good reason." He had the greatest: "I want to be able to argue with my cameramen."

Dean's reasons were less clear. Was he really serious? Did he feel a need to manipulate situations, or did he merely want to record them? Could an actor of his presence record events without influencing them? Twenty-six years later I'm still puzzling over some of the possible answers.

I feel I knew him better than many people but I never knew vast areas of his personality. At once, he was a man with a great emergent talent, a screwball sense of humor, a flair for daredevilry. Yet he held lofty standards for heroic achievement and was intellectually curious. In the years since his death some of him has remained: not only the photographs, not just his fans (who have at times plagued my life), but something of the essence of the creative daredevil I knew, the man who was perpetually both at ease and on guard.

I first met James Dean knowing absolutely nothing about him. Arlene Sax, a young actress friend, called up one winter day in 1954: "I met this wonderful genius—an acting genius! And I want you to meet him." Photographing actors and actresses was a large part of my business, so I was naturally wary of yet another "genius." "Please, Arlene, does it have to be today?"

"Yes," she said. "You see, we're right around the corner . . ."

I groaned.

"I know you're busy, but I promise, we won't stay long, but you've . . . wait till you see his beautiful face!"

So she brought him around to my studio in Manhattan's Murray Hill section. As I opened the door she threw her arms around me and kissed me. I held her at arm's length to look at her dark hair and sparkling eyes. I finally noticed her companion, the guy her kiss was really meant for, standing at a distance.

What a shock. He slouched, was unkempt and squinty. After a moment, he reached for my offered hand, grunted in response to my welcome and ambled to a seat at the far end of the couch. As he sat with his palms pressed between his knees, he seemed to shrivel.

I sat in my usual wing chair, Arlene near me on the couch. She was quite animated as she spoke of his talents: "God, he's magnificent doing that dance in *The Immoralist* . . . You should see him use those scissors as . . ."

"Castanets! Like this," Dean said as he jumped up and performed the dance. It transformed him. The small lump on the couch rose to become a thing of beauty. I couldn't get over how his unpleasant, pinched face gave way to handsome radiance.

Just as suddenly, his face stiffened and contorted, his back stooped into a hump, his legs shortened and his toes turned in. Still performing, he was transformed again, a buffoon who popped out his two front teeth and, lisping, offered his palmed bridge: "Wanna buy thum gold, man? I need thum thoup."

We laughed and laughed, the tension broken. By the time they left, late that afternoon, we were not only friends but he had asked to be my student.

Not long after our first meeting, Jimmy gave Arlene and me tickets to see *The Immoralist*, which was playing at the Royale Theater. The play tells the story of the honeymoon of a French couple in Africa. During the trip the wife discovers that the tropical fever her husband supposedly had was in truth a homosexual affair arranged by a North African wheeler dealer. It starred Geraldine Page, who received an Oscar for the movie *Hondo* that year, and Louis Jourdan, who had made *Letter from an Unknown Woman, Madame Bovary, The Paradine Case* and *Three Coins in the Fountain.* David Stewart played the homosexual lover and James Dean the homosexual procurer. Dean won a Tony and a Daniel Blum award as the most promising actor of the year for his work in the play. That he won the awards that season, that his star shone as it did, is remarkable in retrospect. The theater that year was extraordinary: *Tea and Sympathy,* directed by Elia Kazan, *Dial M For Murder* with Maurice Evans, *The Caine Mutiny* with Henry Fonda, *The King and I* with Yul Brynner, *Picnic, Solid Gold Cadillac,* and *Can Can* all played on Broadway. And James Dean still stood out.

Anyway, it was very rainy the night we saw *The Immoralist* and particularly unpleasant waiting outside the stage door for Geraldine Page and Jimmy. We were meeting to go back to my place for coffee.

Gerry emerged first, greeting us warmly. Then Jimmy rolled out his motorcycle. "Oh, no. Not in this rain," Gerry said. Jimmy wore a diabolic grin as he gunned the motor. He looked at Arlene and yelled, "Get on the back."

She looked at him, then at us, then skyward into the rain, and climbed on behind him. "Oh, Arlene," Gerry yelled, but her words were lost as the cycle roared away.

Standing in the wet and wind I wondered: why was he daring fate when his career was blossoming? At that point I didn't know him well enough to understand that the need to face danger was an integral part of him.

When we stepped out of the cab at my place we expected them to be there. They weren't anywhere in sight as we looked down to Third Avenue in the downpour. In a few moments they appeared and raced by on the motorcycle, laughing and shouting "See yuh." They disappeared around a corner, ignoring our entreaties. They eventually drove by again, having taken a circuitous route around the block. We wondered if they would stop this time. We also wondered how many times they had done the circuit before we had arrived. Like anxious parents, we vowed to brain them when they finally landed.

When they did stop, sweet Gerry hugged and kissed them both. Jimmy looked at me with his shining, wet face, grinning, "Wanna go for a ride, Teach?"

The New York scene in the 50's, at least the one in which I traveled, was fairly casual. We frequented a few favorite restaurants and bars and gathered for informal parties and meals. Being a photographer who operated out of his home and worked with people in the theater, it was natural that my place was often a gathering point.

My studio in the East 30's was—and still is—on the ground floor of an old brownstone. The studio is medium-sized with a fireplace that no longer works, kitchen, bathroom and darkroom. Its special feature is a high-walled garden in back. In the center is a sculptured head from whose mouth water flows into a tiled basin.

The parties that took place there were often fluid, as people moved from the studio to the garden and back again. Jim had a particular fascination for the fountain, and was usually found near it, whether during a party, at a photo class, or just "hanging out."

Our parties usually consisted of a lot of talk and a lot of music, either live or recorded. The talk usually centered around theater and movies—particularly what was playing in the Off-Broadway theaters such as the Circle in the Square, Provincetown Playhouse and the Cherry Lane. Since most of the guests were actors, we talked about not only what plays were around, but about acting schools and teachers that most were associated with, including Berghof, Strasberg, Meisner and Adler. Naturally, we discussed a wide range of plays, too, particularly those of Williams, Hellman, Miller, Ibsen, Chekhov, Coward, Shakespeare and Shaw, quoting and acting scenes from many of their works.

We had plenty of food, beer and soda, usually from delicatessens, and sometimes a roasted chicken from the S & S Rotisserie on Third Avenue. They cost less than a dollar apiece (to match the twenty-five-cent cigarettes and twenty-cent beers).

You never knew just what to expect at a party—when Jim was present the air was always slightly charged. One evening a group of us was listening to music. We had started with Schoenberg and had moved on to blues and jazz—Gershwin, Billie Holliday, Louis Armstrong and Peggy Lee. The turntable became our campfire as we sat around on the floor letting it warm our esthetic innards.

There was one light stand, in a far corner, with a low-watt bulb aimed at the ceiling. A blue haze of cigarette smoke hung in the air. Occasionally, Jimmy tapped quietly on his bongos in time with something Louis or Kid Ory was playing. As Bunny Berrigan's "I Can't Get Started" played, we discussed the "olden days." "Boy, kids were different then," I insisted.

"Shut up!" Jim yelled. "I can't hear the music." He slammed his foot hard on the floor, then crossed his legs again. Jimmy was obviously feeling moody and wanted everyone else to commune with the music as he did.

After a while the talk picked up again. One of the girls complained that men were no longer gentlemen, that they now didn't even take girls home from a date. "Saps!" scowled Jim, re-crossing his legs and resuming his toe-tapping. Someone put on Peggy Lee singing "You Gotta Do Right" as the girls continued talking.

"Okay, okay!" Jim roared suddenly. "Let's hear the goddamned music," he said as he slammed both feet on the floor. The room was instantly silent. "Yuh had plenty money back in twenty-two . . . ," the record continued.

"Play it again, Sam," crooned a girl, finally breaking the silence, and we all, except Jim, quietly sang the *Casablanca* heart-wrencher, "As Time Goes By." Jimmy moved to the big chair with his bongo drum and broke up the end of the song with a different rhythm. He banged it much louder than necessary.

"I love Billie Holliday," a girl yelled over Dean's din. She scowled at him.

"I'm collecting all her records."

"She had a terribly sad life," someone else shouted.

"A wonderfully honest gal."

Dean, obviously feeling ignored, dashed out the door with his bongo drum, like a spoiled child.

The next time I saw him, he arrived at our next get-together as though nothing had happened. He presented me with a Kid Ory record as a kind of apology. You never knew what to expect of him.

While the incident of the bongo was not uncharacteristic, Dean also had an infectiously crazy sense of the absurd. He could be sullen and childish but he could also use his feelings of outrage to create outlandish situations that often bordered on the dangerous.

One evening after a photo session at my place, the usual crew of Marty Landau, an actor who later became known for his "Mission Impossible" television series, Billy Gunn, who understudied Jimmy in *The Immoralist*, Bobby Heller, another actor and student of mine, and I sat around over sandwiches and drinks. It was a while before we noticed that Jim had left us. "Hey, Jimmy," we yelled. No response. "Hey, Jimmy," once again. "Maybe he's sick in the can," someone said. "Hey, Jimmy," yet again.

The next thing we knew there was a hell of a racket out in the street, complete with horns blowing and people yelling. We ran to the window and opened the venetian blind. There, in the middle of the street, sitting cross-legged in my chair, smoking a cigarette, was our boy, holding up traffic.

As we all flew out the front door, we looked beyond the chair and saw a long string of headlights and people getting out of cars. Marty and I grabbed Dean from the chair—and also from a tall, angry-looking guy with big hands who looked ready to pummel him. Jim acted like a rag doll when we pulled him from the chair, his arms and head flopping around, the rest of him just dead weight. Bob and Billy picked up the chair. Once inside, we all looked at the grinning Dean.

"God damn it, Jim," I yelled.

"What do you think you're . . ." Marty began.

Bobby and Billy threw up their hands. "He's gone nuts. Pure, unadulterated nuts."

After I calmed down, I asked him, "Why, Jim, why?"

He took a fresh cigarette and sat in the chair that had been put back in its place. He lighted up and looked at all of us.

"Don't you sons of bitches ever get bored? I just wanted to spark things, man, that's all." He got up and began bongoing the side table.

"Look at you. Before I did it, we were all sitting quietly eating and drinking, and outside a lot of nine-to-fivers were going home to their wives, like they do every night. Now you're all juiced up, and so are they, man. They'll talk about it for years."

Sometimes Dean's put-ons were more subtly calculated. One evening after a party at my place where we had played charades and done impersonations, Jim, Bobby Heller and an actress stayed to help clean up. We made quick work of the task and settled down for coffee, smokes and a critique of the evening. The conversation had moved around, as usual, to plays and movies when the girl commented that there were too few good women's parts. We all agreed and started naming the good ones that came to mind: Scarlett in *Gone with the Wind;* Blanche in *A Streetcar Named Desire;* Regina in *The Little Foxes;* Marguerite in *Camille;* Claire Trevor's part in *Key Largo* (a supporting role, but a memorable performance).

Jim asked me to name my favorite movie with a female lead. Without hesitation I answered *The Heiress* with Olivia de Havilland, and the actress instantly voiced her agreement. It's the story of a plain, unloved but wealthy spinster who is wooed by a cunning fortune-hunter played by Montgomery Clift. Ralph Richardson plays de Havilland's imperious father. As I spoke, Dean's eyes became mischievous. He looked at the actress and said he'd never heard of it, so it must be a bore.

Apparently he read the actress's earnestness right, for she was shocked at his dismissal of the movie. He needled her, saying he was sure it was just a story about a dame with a lot of dough and men running after her. I saw she was uncomfortable and tried to help, saying I thought it was one of the best pictures I'd ever seen.

He looked at me with exaggerated surprise and said, "That's a hell of a lot to say about a movie. It can't be that good."

"Okay, Jimmy Kazan, what makes a good picture?"

Jimmy popped out his front teeth and said: "You mutht thay thomething and mutht thay it differently." The girl laughed and seemed relieved. But Dean wasn't through.

With his teeth back in he offered up the usual cliché about a movie needing a beginning, middle and end. He was floundering, talking about something he had never seen, but he was intent upon getting a rise out of her. He squinted at me while both hands rose up in front of him in a quick two-gun draw, as if he had offered the last word on the subject and he were challenging us.

We protested in unison that that was not all. "What the hell else?" he said, turing up his palms. I could see that there was a grin lurking beneath his surface expression, but nevertheless fell into the trap of pompously expostulating on the art form. He acted hurt that we had protested when I finally finished.

Then he threw an imaginary cape over his shoulder, and said, "Now what about the villains?"

The girl blurted out angrily, "You have the nerve to criticize a picture you've never even seen!"

"Hey, I'm just asking questions," he simpered.

I started again, only to be interrupted by the girl. She was yelling. "I've never seen anything as wonderful as *The Heiress!*"

Jim fell back on the couch, his hands raised to repel any more of the attack. "Okay, okay, I'll see it. I'll see it."

Dean found it fun, getting a response out of people.

Dean seemed to thrive on dangerous stunts, and he used his motorcycle as his instrument more than once.

I always refused to get on the back of it when he drove. "Why," he would ask, "Yuh scared?"

"Yes, Jim, I'm scared," I once answered. "You take too many chances."

We were in front of my place, and he gunned the motor and took off. I would have stopped him and gotten my camera for some shots, but he was already zooming toward Park Avenue.

I went inside. About fifteen minutes later my doorbell rang. I hadn't heard any loud crashes, but was still relieved to find Jimmy when I opened the door.

"That was a short trip," I said and smiled. "Glad to see you back alive."

He headed for the couch and settled in for an argument. He talked about the exhilaration of taking chances and how great that felt. I am by nature more cautious, so our discussion was lively. We finally wound around to bullfighting and Hemingway's *Death in the Afternoon.*

His eyes lit up and he leaned forward as he insisted that "Old Hemingway squeezed the juice out of life."

I agreed.

"I'm not going to live past 30," he said, and smiled, looking intently at me.

During our first meeting Jim asked me if I would shoot him, not as a regular session, but to document his activities. It soon developed that he wanted to shoot me as well, so we began classes. I immediately found out that his concentration was not to be counted on, which meant that our classes were somewhat unpredictable and by necessity changeable in form.

However, when he was interested and participating, his energy was powerful. He had that greatest of intellectual qualities—curiosity about everything.

Dean usually came over to my studio for photography lessons. Sometimes we handled cameras as I taught him the mechanics of picture-taking. Often the heart of a lesson was going outside to shoot. We also spent time in the darkroom developing and printing. I maintain that to understand photography you must be able to make your own photographs from start to finish, and I prefer the control I maintain by doing my own. Jimmy detested the tedium of darkroom work.

It was in the darkroom that we traveled over a wide range of subjects. Dean and I often talked about art to get him through the session. He was particularly curious about people who were able to communicate their perceptions or ideas in a bold or unusual way. We often discussed artists of different disciplines, one time talking about photographers, another time a painter, another a writer.

My background is in art, as well as photography, having been a commercial artist and art director before turning to photography full-time. I was able to change careers completely only when I had become established taking theater production photos, which, in part, I was able to do because I had acting experience.

One day as we emerged from a session in the darkroom, Dean turned to me and asked: "Who are your favorite photographers? The great ones?" I am partial to several, both living and dead, and after running down a list from Matthew Brady to Cartier-Bresson, I settled on Ansel Adams and Edward Weston as the best of the F64 club.

F2 was a basic setting Dean had chosen to work with, and I had drilled its definition into his mind. When I mentioned F64 he grinned like a kid in a school recital as he said: "F2 is when the diameter of the lens goes twice into its focal length when the camera is focused at infinity." He dug his toe into the floor and stuck his fingers in his mouth as he finished, then added, "And practically no depth of field."

I told him about Ansel Adams' "Moonrise," taken with an 8 x 10-inch camera. Every little twig and stone in the foreground and every rock and crevice up to the moon itself is in focus. Then I talked about Edward Weston, the purest of the purists in photography, who sometimes waited for three days before he took one shot of a small rock.

"Why, for Godsake?" shouted Jimmy.

"Weston waited until the shadow was exactly where he wanted it. It was his choice for simplicity of composition."

"One shot?"

"Just one."

Weston's camera for the 8 x 10-inch film was very big and had to be placed on a huge tripod to keep it still enough. After the shot he went back to his darkroom and finished it. Weston didn't use an enlarger. He made a contact print from his 8 x 10 negative by placing an 8 x 10 sheet of sensitized paper, face up, on a table in the dark. He placed his negative, emulsion side down, on the paper, a slightly larger piece of optical glass over that, and then pulled a chain which lit a bare bulb about five feet over the glass for several seconds to expose it.

To Jim there was something heroic about Weston's laborious care and simplicity of technique, so one day, at his insistence, we decided to try out a little of the Weston method. We ventured out before dawn that morning to scout out scenes to shoot. We sat on the edge of the pool in front of the Plaza Hotel as the sun rose. The bright orange light cut a path from the East River straight across 59th Street. Fifth Avenue, empty, looked like an endless striped tie. Its long expanse was deserted but for the whisper and click of a distant vehicle, and a pedestrian here and there.

It was chilly, and though we turned our jacket collars up, we could have used mufflers. We made our way west, across Central Park South, in search of hot coffee and breakfast.

As far as we could see, doormen were hosing down the sidewalk. Several dogs emerged simultaneously from apartment buildings and aimed for the park, dragging their owners. One blond woman in a fur emerged behind a big hound, vainly struggling to keep him, her hair, and her coat under control.

We found a familiar diner on 12th Avenue and sat down at a booth looking out under the West Side Highway at empty piers and over the Hudson River to New Jersey, all of which was awash in the morning light. A small liner cruising down the river completed the scene. A waiter came and took our order.

Jim pulled down his collar and surveyed the diner. "This place reminds me of a Hollywood breakaway set," he mused. Gesturing, he continued. "They'd roll away that half with the coffee urns, and the camera would get here to shoot us and get the booths, the windows and the outside. When they wanted to shoot the counter, this side would roll away for the camera and crew."

After we finished our breakfast, I lighted a cigarette and asked him if he'd found anything to take pictures of.

"Like what?"

"You mean you've forgotten why we took this safari?"

He squinted, then opened his eyes and grinned. "Weston!" he said.

"Right, when are you coming back?"

"Y'know, Teach, I am coming back. I got a kick out of the whole thing—Fifth Avenue, the fountain, the dogs, the walk, and goddamn it, this diner and the way it looks. It'd be a swell place to live."

"Stop kidding. Didn't you see anything to shoot?" I said, exasperated.

"Don't rush me, man. Weston didn't get the camera till he was ready."

As far as I know he was never ready.

If Jimmy hated the labor in the darkroom, he hated most the task of developing negatives. Although he sometimes enjoyed printing pictures if he didn't have to reprint too many times, he found the darkroom confining and requiring too much attention to detail. It was pretty common to hear "The goddamn mother-fucker won't . . . the son of a bitch can't come out right!" Then he would throw the ruined sheet of paper in the can with the others.

One day I scored a great success by getting him to wear an apron in the darkroom. I remember finally putting the loop over his head and tying the bow in back. When he turned around he had his finger in his mouth and his eyes were fluttering. I burst out laughing, right in his face.

Unfortunately, his playful mood didn't last. As the session wore on, and I insisted that he be very careful about temperature and timing to obtain fine grain negatives, he asked why I didn't send my film out to be developed, calling the process "a fuckin' bore, man." His film was in the developing tank, which was in a larger tank of 70-degree water. He lifted the small tank, gave it two jerks for agitation, returned it to the big tank, and looked at the timer. "Two more goddamned minutes."

"You're a child . . . impatient," I chuckled.

He looked at me hard and said he didn't know what I was talking about. Out of pique he suddenly shouted at me to keep quiet. The timer went off. He poured out the developer, rinsed the negatives in the light-tight tank, poured in the hypo, set the timer again and gave the can a couple of jerks. Then he looked at me: "Shit."

I got up and walked into the studio for a cigarette. One of Jimmy's favorite writers was Hemingway, so I yelled back: "Even your daredevil friend Hemingway finds time to be careful."

"He's not my friend," he yelled back. "I never met the son-of-a-bitch."

"No, but you will, if I know you," I screamed.

It was time for coffee, and I headed for the kitchen and started water. Grabbing a box of Oreos and putting it on a table in the studio, I yelled, "No one could construct novels like *A Farewell to Arms* and *The Sun Also Rises* by letting words just fall on pages."

There was a momentary silence and then he shouted, "The masterpieces are on the rack," emerging from the darkroom. "I just put the goddamned fuckers up to dry."

"Take it easy. Hemingway must have had his quiet moments, too," I said, as soothingly as I could.

He stood for a moment with his hands on his hips, snorted explosively, then dug an Oreo from the box. He took off the apron, threw it on the couch and started muttering that "that bearded son-of-a-bitch would be out in Africa shooting tigers or something, man, this very minute, not futzing around with film."

I couldn't help laughing. He smiled, too, as he popped a whole cookie in his mouth and drank his coffee. After swallowing he still insisted: "It's a pain in the ass," but added, "Enough about that. What do you think about Hemingway?"

"Damn fine writer, but continually trying to prove his masculinity makes me doubt him, like Hitler, when he said he could hold his arm in the Nazi salute longer than anyone. Who the hell cares?"

Dean's face looked stricken. I must have hit the center of his holy of holies, his god. The comparison with Hitler was just too much.

"Hemingway is the perfect hero! You can't name anyone as rugged."

There was no point in arguing. Besides, he stalked out, the last word his.

In a way, it was natural that we were at odds, not only when it came to Hemingway, but in basic outlook. His interest was not in carrying something, like photography, from its first step through to its last. He would rather go out and look for a new roost from which to photograph the world, or wait in a car for another to crash head on, just so he could photograph the event. How he would get out of the car wasn't a consideration.

I once told Jim about a successful painter who gave me advice when I was a seventeen-year-old art student. The painter told me to imagine all the artists of the world looking at a building in which something wonderful was happening. Most, he said, would set up their easels at the front door. A few would go to the side and back windows, but the smallest group, perhaps only one person, would find a ladder to reach a small window high up in back.

"You know what I'd do, man," Jimmy interrupted, "I'd get on the roof and drill me a hole—or go to the basement and drill up through the floor."

Jimmy was interested in art and perception. He once demanded that I explain Picasso, so I gave a brief history of his work. He then said, "I guess I really want to know about that period where a guy's face is in profile but you can see both his eyes."

"It's called simultaneous perspective or simultaneity and means seeing an object from several sides at once."

We left it at that, but another afternoon when we were working in the darkroom, watching an image come up in the developing tray, he asked me again about simultaneity.

We finished up quickly and headed out to the studio. I took down John Rewald's *History of Impressionism* and set it on the drawing table in front of us. I paused, feeling that this time, unlike others when an attitude of assumed seriousness was merely a prelude to an often-embarrassing way-out prank, he was sincere. His face was indeed different. He really wanted to learn. I took pleasure in thinking that he thought I knew the answers.

We started at the beginning and spent the rest of the afternoon poring over the book picture by picture, artist by artist. Finally we reached Picasso. Picasso said that painting a face in profile yet seeing two eyes as though you were looking at it dead on—from different perspectives—made the result more unexpected, more exciting. When drawn in line, it gives color even more unusual shapes to work with. The result is like looking at things from two points of view at once, or simultaneous perspective, "Or, Jim boy, simultaneity," I said.

He went over to the couch and laid down. "Whew!" he said, "I think you lost me about forty words ago. Maybe in six months I'll ask you to go over it again."

A few days later we were on the Museum of Modern Art roof terrace with a crowd including Bob Heller, Billy Gunn, Lennie Rosenman, the composer, and Israel Citkowitz. Jim bent over and whispered loudly in my ear, "Simultaneity."

I laughed, "Now?," I asked.

"Yeah, man," he said aloud. "Let's go down."

On the exhibit floor with the Picassos, I showed him "Les Demoiselles d'Avignon" first and explained that it represented three periods: Cubism, African Sculpture and Simultaneity. Then we looked at "The Girl Before a Mirror," "Night Fishing at Antibes," and finally, "Guernica."

"Maybe if I get to be 35, I'll really understand it," he said.

Some time later I watched him rehearse a television show called "The Thief." The plot and circumstances of the show have long since been forgotten, but Jimmy's behavior that afternoon is indelibly etched. He was in a clowning mood which, after a while, the crew found trying. Everyone and everything was in its place: lights, director, assistants, cameramen. But during one take Jim found a prop wig, held it high like a severed head, shouldered a fireplace poker and smiled, the picture of a victorious warrior. Diana Lynn and Mary Astor, also appearing in the show, laughed while actors Paul Lukas and Patrick Knowles scowled. The director looked over at me with my camera poised. Perhaps he thought it was my presence—and my camera—that made Jim crazy.

For the next take, I was off the set aiming my camera at Jim. Once again, all was quiet and everyone was poised. Then Jim turned to face me. He pushed his glasses off to the side, giving the impression of three eyes, and loudly said: "Look, Roy—Picasso."

It was not so much that James Dean came to an intellectual understanding of Picasso's need for experiments in time and perspective. Rather, what made Jimmy so complex a man, and student, was that his understanding came in flashes. When he translated ideas into performance, he understood.

Other aspects of Jimmy's character were revealed in purely social encounters, such as his sitting in the middle of 33rd Street in an armchair and his bad party behavior. He was a paradoxical combination of egomaniac and loner, wanting to be seen yet hiding from the public. As he became well known we glimpsed even more contradictions in his character.

Bobby Heller, Marty Landau, Billy Gunn and I frequented several places at that time, particularly Louie's Tavern at Sheridan Square, the Cromwell Pharmacy in Radio City and Jerry's on 56th Street. Jim liked Jerry's uptown best. Jerry's served him almost as an office. He took most of his phone calls there and I think they even cashed his checks.

Bobby and I took Jim to Louie's a couple of times, but he didn't like the low, dusty ceiling and thought it was too crowded. "Hell, man, you can't see anyone. Nobody wants to get back and look." I think he meant that nobody could get back and look at him.

Louie's was a place where a lot of creative people hung out, and I think that might have made him uncomfortable, too. Even an inkling of competition was difficult for him.

Louie's was right next door to the Circle in the Square Theater, where a remarkably long Off-Broadway run of Tennessee Williams' *Summer and Smoke* had added considerably to their business. It was not unusual to see playwrights like Arthur Miller, Tennessee Williams, Lillian Hellman, or William Inge; the commercial photographer-turned-Hollywood director Howard Zieff (who, incidentally, often used me as a model); the producer and novelist Noel Behn; and quite an assortment of actors and actresses, including one little-known but hard-working actor named Steve McQueen. Louie's was so popular that unless you were a regular you had to stand outside and wait to be allowed in by ones and twos.

One night at Louie's someone recognized me as a friend of Jimmy's. She was a pretty Canadian girl. I liked the way she pushed her honey-colored hair away from her widely-set eyes. Her voice was low and intense. I would have asked her for a date if I had felt I had the slightest chance with her, but instead she begged me to introduce her to a certain nut who now and then called me friend and teacher.

She slid a ten-dollar bill toward me. I looked at the new green note, but didn't touch it. A ten-dollar bill was real coin of the realm then. For seventy-five cents or a buck, you could get Sal back in Louie's kitchen to whip up the god-damnedest veal and pepper sandwich this side of the Via Veneto.

Her voice was calm as she said, "When Jimmy's at your place, all I want you to do is to give me a call. I don't care what time, day or night. As long as he's there, and if you'll introduce me to him as though I was a friend of yours—casually like it was a natural introduction."

"Then I guess you'd want me to leave so that you could be alone with him?"

"Oh, no," she whispered. "I don't want it to be obvious in any way. Just introduce us, then he might . . . oh, I'll take it from there."

I smiled and tried to think of something to say. Finally, I told her, "It's impossible." Even if I had taken her money and done what she asked, Jimmy would have sensed it as a set-up. I told her I would feel like a liar and could only suggest that she go to Jerry's or Cromwell uptown where she might bump into him. She picked up the dough and left.

I told Jim about her the next day. "Hell, I'd like to date her myself," I said.

"Be my guest," he grinned.

When acting, you must always be in character. As yourself, you might be embarrassed at saying or doing certain things that a character is able to do comfortably. I have come to believe in the years since his death that Jim was almost always in character. I think he let himself "peek out" the day we discussed Picasso at length. Occasionally, he let the mask slip. But rarely.

One day he asked me if I enjoyed acting. I answered yes, but that I wasn't very good and hoped that in the years since I had been on stage I had learned more. I told him that I gave a kind of acting lesson each time I did a sitting. I also got a little impatient, and told him that of all people he should know it, after I took all those portraits of him.

Then he asked me why he and Brando were often compared. I gave him the obvious answer about his character in *Rebel Without a Cause* and Brando's in *The Wild Ones:* both were rebellious, anti-establishment characters. I also told him that maybe part of it was publicity, plain and simple, and that someone might have figured that Dean could cash in on Brando's success.

Jim faced me without anger, and said, "I don't want that kind of help." I regretted my comment immediately, as he looked genuinely hurt. His character cracked, for just a second, and the vulnerable being underneath shone through.

Jim was briefly in the Actors Studio, which in the 50's became well known not only for its illustrious members, but for the way they taught acting. Young actors studied the Method, which requires an actor to identify the reactions and feelings of a character and then personalize them.

When I think about or teach acting I always remember my grandmother's pickles. When I visited her as a child, I always rushed out to her fire escape first thing to dig into her pickle barrel. When she died, I couldn't eat pickles for at least six months. To this day, pickles mean Grandma and I eat them with proper appreciation. As an actor, if I needed a perfect inner action for sadness I would use that recollection as sense and emotion memory.

I believe Marty Landau once said that Dean was filled with the Method. If one of his characters was sick he would actually want to vomit on camera.

One day we were talking about preparing for a part. All of a sudden Jim became the young homosexual in *The Immoralist*. He danced his "castanet/scissors" dance and said. "You gotta give it everything." Finishing the dance, he seated himself tentatively on the sofa, miming, as he put his "castanets" near the camera. "Every part of you's gotta be in there pitchin'— every inch of you, every second. When Brando was doing Stanley Kowalski, he didn't let down once. Man, he was great."

At times he seemed almost obsessed with Brando. Occasionally, for no apparent reason, he would begin quoting from *A Streetcar Named Desire*. One time, during a discussion of Method acting, he took off his shirt and ripped his undershirt to shreds, yelling "Stella!" in imitation of Marlon Brando as Stanley Kowalski yelling for his wife.

He often said, each time as if I'd never heard it, "I had a motorbike before he did."

Jimmy enjoyed taking pictures. He liked to shoot Marty in particular. One night, after an evening at my place, Jimmy started working on Marty. He said to me: "Have you ever noticed Marty's mouth?"

"What do you mean?" I looked at Marty and back to Jim.

"I wanna get real close to it, man."

"You could use a proxar," I said, "but his face would look disfigured. The nearest part would be distorted in relation to . . ."

"That's what I want," sang Jimmy. The resultant shot was one of his most successful and which I later dubbed "Steeplechase," after a gaping-mouth ride at Coney Island Amusement Park.

Jimmy used Marty often. One afternoon he had him lie on his West 68th Street stoop for a series of "dying" shots. He shot Marty and I shot Jimmy shooting Marty.

We were bound for Jimmy's apartment. As we walked upstairs, I noticed the 25-watt bulb in a bracket on the wall. I told him to stand near it. He looked at me as though I were mad. "Yuh kidding. In this light? You're nuts, man. It's too damn dark!" He started to move on but I grabbed him and held him where I wanted him.

"Stand over there! This is part of your class."

Marty laughed, "Teacher's talking."

"But Roy, it's like that black cat in a coal bin at midnight you told me about that no one can find." He protested, but stood still.

"Now feel the wall with your back," I quietly commanded.

"What's your goddamn exposure going to be?"

"Be quiet and take a breath. . . . now let it out slowly," I said, camera at my eye. "Close your eyes for a second. . . . now allow them to open a bit and think of the smell of a rose." . . . Click.

I took a few more, then he grabbed the camera with the F2 lens from me and pushed Marty to the wall, had him put his arm under the light, his face sort of profiled so as not to repeat what I had done. I had taken him full face, his arms at his sides. "I can hold a tenth of a second if you can," he said.

"Hold your breath as you shoot," I warned. The 25-watt photo of Dean was so successful it has appeared in at least a dozen magazines and on the cover of Bill Bast's biography.

Jimmy's apartment was one small room measuring about eight by ten feet. It had one round window set high in the wall over his bookshelves. There was a tiny bathroom. Bull horns and a toreador cape hung over a double bed placed to the left of the window. The bull horns and the round window attracted me immediately.

I was anxious to shoot and asked him to stand on the bed so that his head was near the horns. I then pulled the cape over his shoulders. He brought his hands together and grinned. . . . Click. Marty removed the lamp shade and acted as lighting technician. Then Jim took shots of Marty using the same props while I did the lighting.

When they finished I couldn't wait to get Dean in the heart of the round window for some shots. I used just daylight, and opened the window, which added another circle to the compositions. Jim's reflection in the glass and the marrying curves worked beautifully. I believe the results are some of my best compositions.

Next I moved him to a little balcony outside the window. While shooting he asked me if I had ever read *The Little Prince*. We didn't pursue it, but apparently sitting on the balcony reminded him of the little prince whose pride for a special flower made him lose his serenity.

One day we went to Ratner's on Second Avenue for cheese blintzes. We smeared the insides with cream cheese, even though the waiter grimaced and shrugged, saying, "Cheese on cheese?" (Jimmy once put ketchup on a peanut butter sandwich, too).

As we walked home we noticed a candy stand on a side street.

"Watch this," Jimmy said, walking over to it. An elderly woman customer stood in front. Jim looked at me as if to say "Ready?"

I nodded, my camera to my eye.

He picked up a bag of Jets from the outside shelf, not to steal them, but to prove he could and have it on film. Then he sat down on a huge Coca Cola cooler and stared at the customer. She looked at him and then away, repeating the action several times. He kept staring. About the fifth time she leaned over to the unseen attendant and pointed at Jim.

He kept his expression as he slid off the box and walked away.

Dean was just becoming known when I began photographing him. He had done some television work and had finished filming *East of Eden*. Before he filmed *Rebel Without a Cause* he was a hot property. *Life* was the important magazine to appear in at the time and, naturally, Jimmy wanted to be in it. He asked me to show them my shots. Frank D. Campion, the man to see, liked the photos, but said he wanted a serious, more manly sitting. What *Life* wanted we were more than happy to provide.

The day I shot the photos, the session went extraordinarily well. After a certain amount of horsing around, Jimmy behaved and became serious when I got the lighting set just right. He clicked, I clicked, and the photos clicked. He now had quite a bit of photographic experience himself, and after a while I allowed him to direct some of the shots. It was all pretty heady. At one point he commented, "Don't you think I look like Michelangelo's *David*?"

The pictures from that sitting became the "Torn Sweater" series. *Life* magazine, as it turned out, had an exclusive contract with a big agency and couldn't use the pictures I had taken. But to this day, the "Torn Sweater" series are the best known and most popular shots of Dean in the world, even though *Life* never published them.

One day Jim showed up expensively dressed in tailored tan trousers and handmade boots. He had never cared how he looked before, but now he was resplendent. He also seemed to have gotten over a romantic loss and was himself. But money seemed to be burning a hole in his pocket.

"Leave your camera here, Teach. No work, and tell me what restaurant you want to eat at. Make it an expensive one."

"Well, you're becoming a man of the world. I'll be pleased to accept. Let me think. Ah, Luchow's! I haven't had their sauerbraten for a while. Ever been there?"

"Nope," he said, as he doused his cigarette and lit another.

I was sitting on the couch and after he paced around he sat in the wing chair and crossed his legs. "This guy in Hollywood—he's a friend of mine. He's a cameraman and showed me a lot of things." He rubbed his new boots lovingly. "And now I want to make a movie."

I laughed. "Just like that."

"Yeah, I can do it," he argued. "Anyway, I'd like to try."

I continued laughing, "God, you know what it takes?"

"Sure, I learned a lot. I watched him. It's no big deal." He rose and his hands formed a frame, palms out and thumb tips touching, his eyes squinting behind his raised hands. "You put what you want in a frame." He walked towards me and stopped, then squatted an inch or so, the frame still on me.

"Turn your head slowly," he directed. "No, the other way." "Now scratch your ear." I scratched.

"It's a cinch!" he said, his arms flying apart. I put my hands up and framed him, "Look, Mr. Cinematographer, it comes expensive. It means a good 16 mm camera and accessories, extra lenses, film, meter, tripod, developing—it'll run into thousands."

He would not be stopped. We went to a camera shop and bought him a Bolex and the rest of the abracadabra that would soon have his friends cursing him under their breath.

Marty, Billy and Bobby were enthusiastic at first, but after lugging lights, tripod and camera, long wires and innumerable props, we became a little disillusioned. There was no script, unless it was in his head. He seemed most intent on experimental shots and momentary inspirations. At one moment he was crawling under couches while he shot us, at another scrambling toward the one who was acting. He found he could tilt the camera directly up, so 'the actor' stood on a chair bowing from the waist. Dean could then shoot him from below, while the other two lighted him from each side, making crossed shadows on the ceiling.

To top it off, we had a midsummer heat wave. Even in the garden behind my studio, the heat was killing. Our director became enamored of the sculptured fountainhead. We were stripped to the waist and sweating as Jim directed us. "Marty, can I have that light here?"; "Bob, bring over that chair!" Jim had no long ears and whiskers: his upper body was shiny and his bespectacled face was topped with sandy hair. But in that heat my mind bent a little and his commands sounded like Lewis Carroll's White Rabbit saying, "Mary Anne, bring me my gloves and fan." The bright lights and our loud voices brought a lot of heads popping out of nearby windows.

Though he worked us hard for several weeks, to my knowledge no one ever saw the finished product. However, his itch to direct led us into something called "Illustrative Photography." It's a wide field and the shots can be used for mystery magazines, nudie magazines, or any other type of magazine.

He posed me in a bathroom doorway for one of his "Illustrative" shots. Past my head, the mirror reflected a dagger in my hand up against the wall. After describing it, I asked Bob to shoot Jimmy shooting me. The sneaky dagger came out fine, but as a heavy, I'm afraid I look like a frightened villain about to be sick. It could have worked it we'd mixed his direction and my acting better.

Soon after, we found ourselves faced with "lucky news shot photography." We had enjoyed the Plaza Hotel morning, and we chose another sunny day to do the Village. We were on Fifth Avenue near the Washington Square arch. Jimmy seemed eager for anything, fortified with all my do's and don'ts and me to double-check him.

A building was going up and we started through a rough-hewn arcade—the temporary structure they put around an area before tearing down or erecting something. As we came out the other side we saw a melée of several policemen and others. We had heard the commotion before we could see it and instinctively grabbed our hanging cameras. As we came out, some of the combatants were down, some up. All were flailing away with their fists. There were no guns drawn yet.

Jim and I clicked away, squatting and getting up on top of things. The crowd was standing back, but we pushed through and got in as close as we dared. One guy on the ground was bleeding pretty badly. As the cuffs were being put on him, Jim shot some good close-ups while I shot him shooting. I went back to my shots, capturing a fist connecting with a cop's face, causing his hat to fly off. It was all over quickly when more cops came. The corner became calm again.

We couldn't wait. We cabbed fast to my place to develop our masterpieces, but as we walked to the darkroom, Jim had a strange look on his face. He glared at his camera.

"You know," he said, "I don't think I took my lens cap off. Christ, I'm sure I didn't."

I couldn't laugh, it was too painful. I opened my camera to take out the film. Maybe I looked a little smug. I remember him watching me as I put my lens cap back on in the cab. I had learned the lens cap lesson painfully once when not only did I leave my cap on, but I had to read about it in a newspaper.

Leo Shull had a successful newspaper out on Fire Island. In it, he had a column and he naturally mentioned arrivals, departures, and activities of the many Manhattanites who ferried out on the weekends. His prize piece on a certain weekend was: "Roy Schatt, famous theatrical photographer, was seen on the beach yesterday in the beautiful sunlight, immortalizing all and sundry . . . *with his lens cap on.*"

Jimmy watched me as I reached for the film spool in the camera.

"Oh my God! There's no film in the camera!"

We cursed, but soon there was nothing to do but laugh. We laughed loud and long. We laughed until we were flat on our backs panting for air. I told him about the Leo Shull column and we laughed some more.

As Jim's fame rose we could no longer walk nonchalantly around town or spend a couple of hours on the roof terrace of the Museum of Modern Art. People turned and stared as he passed.

My shots of him were well known, too, which associated me with him. In 1954, before he really became famous, I must have answered over a hundred phone calls for James Dean. Apparently his television work had turned on a number of gushy girls. At first, it was kind of fun. Occasionally he was there when one phoned. He saw me touch my forehead, close my eyes and sigh. He would giggle as he heard me gently get rid of them. A few times I got even with him and directed them to his usual hangouts. Once he heard me do it, and grabbed the phone and slammed it into its cradle. He avoided his favorite places for a while.

Once when Dean wasn't around, a pretty girl came to ask me about doing her portraits. She looked about twenty and was very carefully made up. She quietly asked me the right questions and we set up an appointment for the following week. As we talked, her eyes roamed the apartment. They were small movements, but I could see her mind was not on the appointment with me.

I finished a remark, ". . . and no more than three changes."

"Uh, what?"

"Only three changes of outfit . . . costume."

"Uh, I don't want . . . changes." She got up and walked to the french doors, which she opened, then leaned out to case the garden. She straightened up and stood in front of me.

"Where is he?" she demanded.

"Who?" I asked innocently.

She went quickly into the kitchen, then into the other two rooms and came back to me.

"I thought I saw him come in the building a while ago. I know he lives here."

"You mean James Dean?"

"Who else?"

"There's a guy upstairs—same color hair. You probably saw him. Dean is my student, but he lives somewhere else. I don't expect him today."

"What!" she screeched, two octaves above the voice she'd been using. It cut five years off the twenty I'd originally guessed.

"You're about fifteen," I said.

"Well . . ." Her face was red and damp.

"And you don't really want pictures, do you?"

She turned to the door and I quickly let her out.

I complained to Jim once about his fans' phone calls and visits.

"What do you want me to do, man?" he laughed.

"Do they phone you at your place, Jim?"

"Only my friends know my number. Everyone knows yours."

I was getting angry. "I ought to gather a couple of dozen of them and drop them in your lap."

"Aw, c'mon. Don't some of them get to be your customers?"

"This may surprise you, but none of them does."

He put his hands on the back of his head, got up on his toes and moved around in a small circle like a ballet dancer. He looked at the floor and said, "Can't do . . . anything . . . about . . . it." He came down flat on his feet, looked at me and said, "I'm sorry." Then he added, "They're girls . . . stupid silly *girls*." I suspect that his outburst bespoke less of his sexual tastes than of his difficulty in handling his celebrity.

One evening he called, asking to come down. I was with a date.

"It'll be okay in about an hour, Jim."

After putting down the phone I looked at my date. Her eyes glistened and she smiled.

"Can't I stay and meet him?"

"My God, isn't there a sane female in this town?"

"What's wrong with meeting him?" she said, a little insulted.

"Nothing, nothing at all, only you're just one of a couple of million. Every girl in the world wants to meet him."

I lowered my voice and said: "Won't you feel the least bit embarrassed? He knows you've been with me. Anyway . . ." I gestured dramatically, "he likes to start a relationship."

"Who the hell said anything about a relationship?"

She finally left and shortly Dean came stalking in like Groucho Marx. He opened closet doors and looked behind clothes. "Maybe in the kitchen?" he sneered at me as he sashayed all the way to the stove and then out again. "There's more than one way to kill a cat," he said as he moved to the bathroom. "That's if you like cats," he called over his shoulder.

He was still Groucho when he emerged, but I grabbed him and sat him down.

"Stop it, you maniac." Then I pulled my hand away. "God, you're wet."

"That's sweat, man. I walked down."

He started to take his clothes off. "Can I take a shower?"

"Sure, and by the way, you do a lousy Groucho," I said as I went to the kitchen.

"Thanks. Where are you going?"

"To make milkshakes," I shouted from the refrigerator.

Soon I heard knocking on my door. I went and opened it and there was Dean, under the front hall light, bare-ass naked. I imagined the Thornes, the two seventy-year-old ladies who lived above me, coming down the stairs at that moment. Or any of my other neighbors, for that matter. I pulled him in and threw him on the couch.

"You stupid son-of-a-bitch. You nincompoop," I yelled.

He was now stretched out like one of those western paintings that hung over saloon bars, one hand over his crotch, the other across his breast. He was giggling like a virgin with pursed lips and fluttering eyes. Then he sat up and really laughed.

"Boy, you should see your face."

Jimmy gay? Or bisexual? Well, maybe. His nuttiness and constant attempts at breaking from the humdrum could have led him into it.

A group of us was eating at an Italian restaurant in the Village one evening, a couple of blocks from the Circle in the Square Theater. A girl came in and plunked herself down on Marty Landau's lap. She hugged and kissed him, told him how wonderful he was, and how long she'd been after him. Marty's look was of disbelief. You could tell that he'd never met her. Then Jimmy jumped up and leaned over the table yelling, "Stop it, don't do it with him. It's me you should be making love to, I'm the star. I'm the important one. I've been in a movie and a play. It's me you should be kissing."

Jimmy kept raving about himself, but after the girl gave him a quick look, she went back to kissing Marty, who by this time was enjoying every minute of it.

After a couple of minutes, Dean didn't seem to care anymore—it was just another of his put-ons.

Once, on the roof of the Museum of Modern Art, a group of us was discussing good-looking movie stars, particularly Montgomery Clift and Marlon Brando. A girl nearby added "And Jimmy Dean." Jim was there, of course, and he stood up, twisted his head to give us his profile against the sky, turned back to us and took his teeth out and crossed his eyes. We all laughed, except the girl. Her face turned red with embarrassment as she stared at him. He put his teeth back in and threw her a kiss, which seemed to calm her down enough for her to be able to smile.

Another day, we walked up Park Avenue to lunch. The day before he had accused me of cashing in on his celebrity. He quickly apologized when he saw my anger, but my mood lingered. He had pressured me to come to lunch with him the next day, and I finally agreed.

We were outside the Waldorf Astoria Hotel and he was pretending to be a war correspondent when he saw two proper young women wearing gloves and hats emerge from the hotel. They were obviously tourists and they noticed him at the same moment that he noticed them. They stopped dead with their mouths open.

He continued walking towards them, feeling adventurous, his bouncy, arrogant body like a not-yet-tamed terrier, overfondled and under-spanked. He was on, and aware of his every action. He had a season ticket to tweak the nose of the world.

He was no longer the war photog as he walked towards them: he was now an autograph seeker and, in his anxious speed, put on the brakes only inches from their faces.

"May I take your pictures?" he pleaded. He took several shots as he moved briskly around them, saying, "Oh, that's good! Now look across the street, now at each other. Thank you. Thank you, very much." He then grabbed my arm and walked me up the avenue.

His giggle grew into a laugh as we marched away. I asked him what he was laughing at. He yelled something through his laughs, but I couldn't understand it. Finally, after a breath, I got it.

"There's no film in the camera!"

"Why, for God's sake?"

He clicked the empty camera at the girls, who were now about a block away, then squatted as he clicked the unloaded machine up into my face.

"It's a surrealist joke, like Dali's soft watches that can't work, yet tell the goddamned time, man."

He aimed the camera at two sour-faced tourists who were staring at him from a horse-drawn carriage and said, "It's dear old Dali, Dali with a fringe on top."

I think the real reason for not loading his camera was his special apology to me, since I wouldn't carry a camera that day. That way, if he saw things he wanted to photograph, he wouldn't be able to shoot them. It was a creative apology.

There was a side of Jim I saw only once. He went out to California to film *East of Eden,* and when he returned he called, asking for a class. As soon as he arrived I knew something had changed. He seemed subdued and preoccupied. He wasn't really interested in a class, so we talked of other things instead. Throughout the conversation the name Pier popped out in comments such as, "Oh, I enjoyed the trip, but Pier said . . . ," the rest of the sentence trailing off. I couldn't tell whether Pier was a man or woman, but it seemed like a romantic preoccupation.

As we talked, he sighed, looked at the clock several times, then at his hands, then at me.

"Can I make a call to Hollywood—it'll be collect. She's expecting it."

"Sure," I said, reaching for the phone near the desk.

"No, I'd like to make it in the darkroom."

"Go ahead."

He moved quickly there and closed the door. Soon from behind it his voice rose in spurts like a tiny machine gun.

"Hey, Roy! Come here!" It was like a little boy's cry in the wilderness.

I went in. He was standing straight, facing me and offering me the phone. He was blushing. I had never seen that look. His eyes seemed larger and sadder than they'd ever been and just about to spill over.

"Here," he said. "Tell her. Tell her where I am." Then he closed his eyes and opened them. "Oh, yes, Roy, this is Pier Angeli."

"Hello, Pier."

"Hello, Roy. I hope you don't . . . Roy, please tell Jimmy not to get so excited."

"I'll do that," I said and handed the phone back to him. "She said not to get excited."

I left him and closed the door.

When he came out he said little, but asked for a glass of water. Then he left.

I soon found out that one of their big problems had been Pier's mother. She didn't approve of Jimmy: his manners, his clothes, his hair, his fast driving, his not being a Catholic. He had tried to spruce up, wearing ties and having his shoes shined, but it was apparently not a relationship meant to be. Eventually he got over it and resumed his normal behavior, but the incident was unique. Not only did I glimpse a depth of feeling in him, but it was the first time I had ever seen any indications of his emotional self beyond the manifestations of his crazy and dangerous behavior.

Jimmy had been in California about a month when news came that he had died in a car crash. His mania for taking chances, for shocking us and generally fracturing the normal way of things seemed always to be simmering. It must have been with him throughout his life, and certainly with him on that California highway when he pushed his Porsche to 65 MPH in a 45 MPH zone. I must admit that the final irony is that he slowed down and it became the other driver's fault.

God, it was a shock. I could only think of how alive he was, remember him quickly grabbing an elusive thing and making it part of an exciting moment. He hadn't been the kind of friend one could count on or whose actions you could predict, but he had a constant vitality rarely found in people.

For one moment after I heard of his death, don't ask me why, I smiled. I felt lousy, but I smiled and thought of Noël Coward's ending to *Blithe Spirit* in which his delightful characters crash their car, die, and immediately return as ghosts sitting on a nearby fence. Jimmy, I realize now, did the same thing. I had no way of knowing at the time that interest in James Dean and my involvement with him was not at an end. It has always puzzled me that he has become such a popular and almost mythical figure, spawning cult groups all over the world.

One of the places we hung out in the 50's was the Cromwell Pharmacy on the ground floor of the RCA building at Radio City. At the time it was known as the city's largest drugstore. For all its other goods, its main attraction was its eating area, a large space that took up most of its center.

It was called by some the "poor man's Sardi's." The office building over the pharmacy houses the radio and television studios of NBC, where more shows were broadcast in the mid-50's than can now be accounted for by NBC's program analysts themselves. Milton Berle's "Texaco Star Theater," the Goodyear, Philco and Kraft playhouses were all broadcast from there. Many working actors, along with those looking for work, showed up around two or three o'clock in the afternoon to brag a little, chat, and relax.

I delivered photos there one afternoon to an actor who was with a group of friends. They filled three tables in the northwest corner of the dining area. I was greeted by Louie Guss and Leonardo Cimino (both of whom later appeared in *The Godfather*), along with several others. After finishing business, I sat, ordered coffee and surveyed the place.

The dark wood wainscoting that surrounded the tables had a few nondescript framed 8 x 10s of NBC performers hung randomly. My mind's eye envisioned the wood covered with homosote, painted white, and displaying my work with well-mounted 14 x 17s and 16 x 20s.

A shortish man with a moustache walked over and began looking at my photos which had been passed around the actors' tables. It was Mr. Beck, Cromwell's owner, and he soon came over and asked me if I would like to exhibit there.

Soon the white-painted homosote was in place, displaying about 100 Schatt portraits. Cromwell's must have been pleased, for I was given coffee on the house whenever I wished. I often updated the exhibit, and it ran for several years, during which time I had some interesting experiences.

I became an observer at the Actors Studio, where I was able to meet and photograph rising stars, which gave the Cromwell show particularly contemporary portraits. There were always one or two new James Dean shots when the display changed.

The Dean cult had risen by 1956. People had taken pilgrimages to his home in Fairmount, Indiana, and to the cemetery where he was buried. Many groups formed, not only in the U.S., but as far away as Germany and Teheran. In Jakarta, Indonesia, kids started wearing blue jeans and red jackets, the symbolic costume from *Rebel Without a Cause.*

One day over coffee in the Cromwell, I was looking at the "Torn Sweater" shot of Dean when I noticed a blond kid sitting a few stools away. He was wearing a black turtle-neck sweater like the one in the photo. Kids had imitated Jim before. Sometimes they walked towards me in the street with his grimace and slouch and a cigarette hanging from a limp hand. Then they'd look quickly to the side, moving the other hand in the carelessly flopping way of Dean's, then look back at me squinting through the cigarette smoke. Some were damn good. But my God, after seeing dozens of them I felt I was judging a James Dean imitation contest.

Now here was another one. I should have noticed his entrance, I guess, or the way he got onto the stool. His far hand drooped, supported by the elbow on the counter. His near hand was being warmed by the coffee cup. When he wanted to sip, he brought the drooping hand to his lips, allowing the pinky and the third finger to take the cigarette from his mouth as the thumb and first finger of his warmed hand grabbed the ear of the cup to bring it mouthward. Holding it with both hands, he raised his head and sighed, then turned and looked at me under his brows.

That under-the-brows bit did it. I moved to the stool beside him, saw him wince and put his cup down. His eyes had a slight touch of alarm.

"Look," I said, my voice low and annoyed. "Why the hell don't you do yourself a favor?"

"What'ya mean, man. You crazy?"

I looked at him steadily.

"You'll never make it as James Dean, but you stand a good chance of making it as yourself."

I had rarely found myself in such a position of power. I felt that if I pushed harder, he would either cry or stiffen and sock me. We stood our respective bits of ground for a moment, then he sat up straight and a sigh rose from deep within him. Our eyes were on a level. Then came a grin which blossomed into a very original smile—not a bit like Jimmy Dean.

"Glad to meet you, Mr. Schatt," he said as he reached out his hand. "I just wondered if I could do it."

"Do what?"

"Make you see a ghost," he said as he got off the stool and left the pharmacy. He showed up later at my place for a sitting.

Over the years my photos of Jim have appeared in magazines and been seen all over the world. TV movies have used my stills of him. The best-known shot of the "Torn Sweater" series was used not only as a backdrop for the stage revue *Grease,* but also on six- and twelve-sheets outside of theaters. They've also been printed as posters in all sizes and been sold in novelty and gift shops. Naturally, my name has become associated with those photos, and with it have come some rather odd occurrences.

For eleven years I was part of a permanent panel on "The Long John Nebel Radio Show," heard in the New York area from midnight until four in the morning. It was a call-in show, and the subjects ranged from flying saucers to floating kidneys. On every show at least one person asked me about James Dean.

People often came to my studio, hunting for a bit of Dean or just the knowledge that he had been there to take with them.

A few years ago, a fan from South Africa visited me to buy photos of Dean. The week before another came from Japan, and the month before one came from Australia. Many from closer locales came, too.

The cultists were really something. One day a girl arrived on my doorstep in tears. The throb in her throat and minor key of her voice told me she had it bad. Her voice droned until I placed the photos in her lap. Then her eyelids dropped and her voice caught a high note as a small tear appeared as she gently fingered the top portrait in the pile.

I watched her as I had many others. From everywhere, they had come to sit in the room he had sat in, with photos of him on their laps. They then moved to the wing chair and each one carefully picked a thread from an ever-increasing hole, reverently stowing it away. After they had chosen their photos they would squeeze my hand as if to say, "The funeral will go on and on," and then show up some time later for more photos.

I really don't understand why after all these years and countless exhibits that included portraits of Marilyn Monroe, Paul Newman, Eva Marie Saint, and many, many more, the only photos that were ever stolen from the walls were those of James Dean. At one point I had lost so many that I put a quarter-inch plastic shield over the most popular "Torn Sweater" shot. My effort was in vain. I don't know how someone managed to pry off the six two-inch screws, but they did. I've now stopped exhibiting his portraits.

One aspect of the cult fascination took an interesting turn when *Motion Picture* magazine asked me to be hypnotized to bring Jim back from "the other side." They felt I would be the perfect medium. Wouldn't it be wonderful to have him talk through me to all who loved him, they said.

I told them I'd give it a shot, even though I don't believe in it. I have always laughed at those who say they've talked to the dead. Others had tried to hypnotize me, but it had always failed. The people assured me that the hypnotist they would use was the very best.

They were so confident of the experiment that they welcomed my suggestion to bring along two observers. Bobby Heller, Marty Landau and I arrived at the appointed time at the New Yorker Hotel. We greeted the assorted entourage, including the professional hypnotist, who looked at me with scorn. Her smile said, "You'll be a pushover."

Like a set, everyone was ready and in place, and the show began. "Your eyelids are heavy and you must close your eyes . . . you must close your eyes . . . and you want to close your eyes," she repeated in a sing-song voice. My eyes stayed bright and alert. She commanded that I close my eyes. I was wide awake. She droned, I sat. Finally, after what seemed an eternity, she lost patience.

"Oh, you, you, you're not cooperating, not even trying."

She stalked out in a boiling rage.

Jimmy would have said: "That dame could use a hell of a lot of acting lessons, man."

To this day, I can sometimes hear his comments and imagine his reactions and I often think of one evening in particular. We had just finished a meal and were smoking while coffee brewed. I studied my pipe and he stared ahead as streams of thin blue smoke rose from the cigarette in his mouth over his eyes and around his head, mixing with my pipe smoke and finally drifting upward. I watched a smile grow on his lips; the angle of his cigarette barely changing. It moved to his eyes, but he crinkled his eyelids into slits almost obscuring the dark blue behind them. He then asked me why my pipe was caked with crud and I told him it made the smoke taste sweeter. I asked why he had a cigarette resting over his left ear and he explained that he would light it "as soon as I'm finished this one, man. But it's really there for you to ask about." We both smiled.

# Photographs

The following pictures were taken primarily from February through December of 1954. During that time I documented Dean's activities and taught him photography. Some of his shots are included and are so marked. Shown are many of the places we frequented: the Museum of Modern Art, my studio, Dean's apartment, various restaurants, television and rehearsal sets.

Jim liked the first walking shot so much that he insisted on a second, this time posing as "The Photographer."

Marty Landau, Jim and I were walking when
Jim suddenly jumped over a rail and began
shooting us from an angle he thought no one
else would use. He shot us and I shot him
shooting us (*following pages*).

*James Dean*

Dean shooting Marty Landau "dying" on Dean's doorstep.

Dean hamming in front of a candy stand, pretending to steal candy for the benefit of the camera. He stared down a customer, then posed for a more serious shot nearby (*following pages*).

Shooting each other in the darkroom.

Jimmy listening to a photography lesson.

Between bites at Minetta's Tavern, Dean shoots a stranger.

We shoot each other, the only available subjects during a lesson (*following pages*).

*James Dean*

*James Dean*

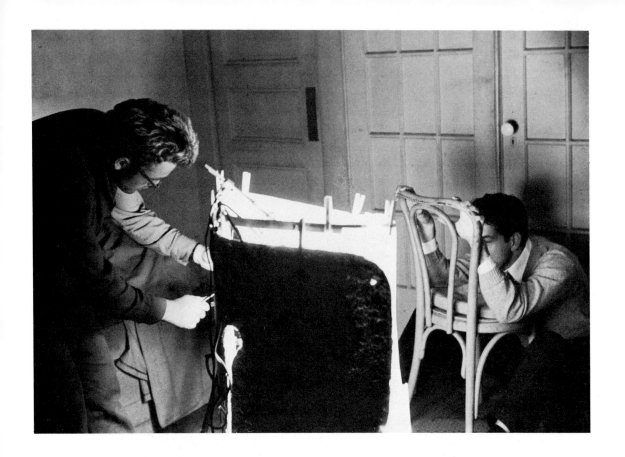

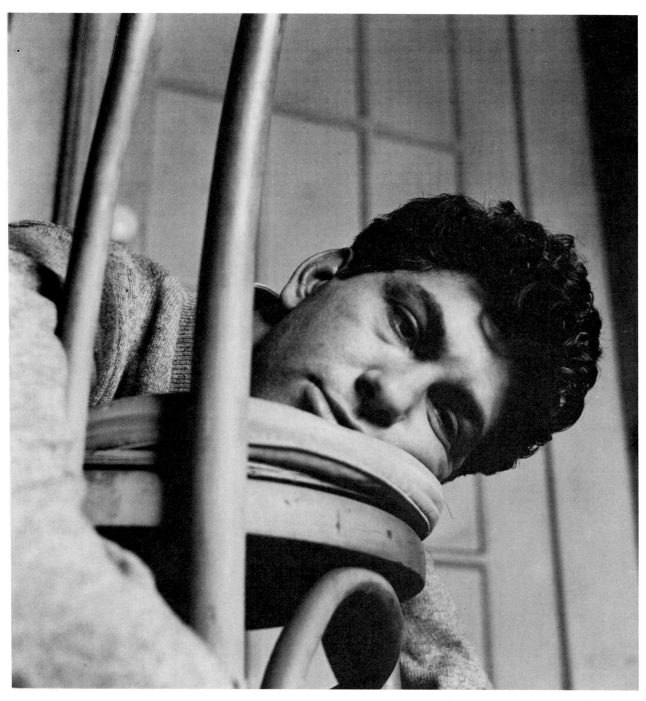

*James Dean*

A photography evening at my place. First Dean sets up and shoots Bob Heller, then Marty Landau, producing a shot I later dubbed "Steeplechase" (p. 75).

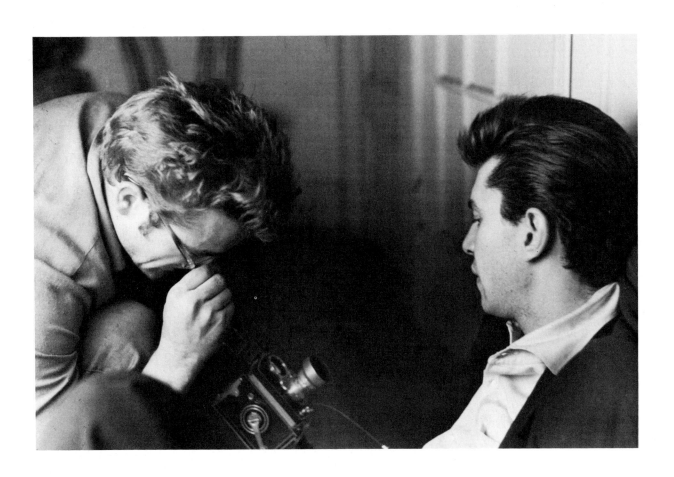

*James Dean*

*James Dean*

Dean was convinced that
my shot of him under a
25-watt bulb couldn't turn
out, yet he grabbed the
camera from me and shot
Marty under it.

*James Dean*

Shooting at Dean's place. Jim makes fun of bullfighting, a
favorite symbol. The cape makes an interesting face profile on
the wall.

He liked the horn effect so well he tried the same shot with Marty. Then I had him sit in the window and took some of my best compositions (*following pages*).

*James Dean*

*James Dean*

*James Dean*

Dean shot me in front of Howard Zieff's ad using my picture.

*James Dean*

*Bob Heller*

*Bob Heller*

*Bob Heller*

Christmas Day, 1954, at my place. Bob Heller shoots me shooting Jimmy.

James Dean portrait of Billy Gunn (*opposite*).

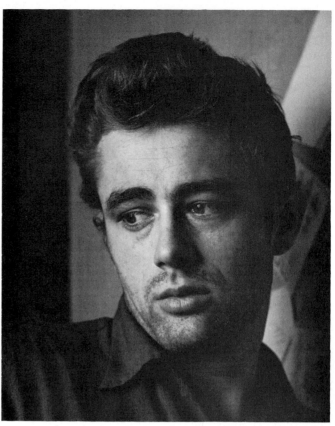

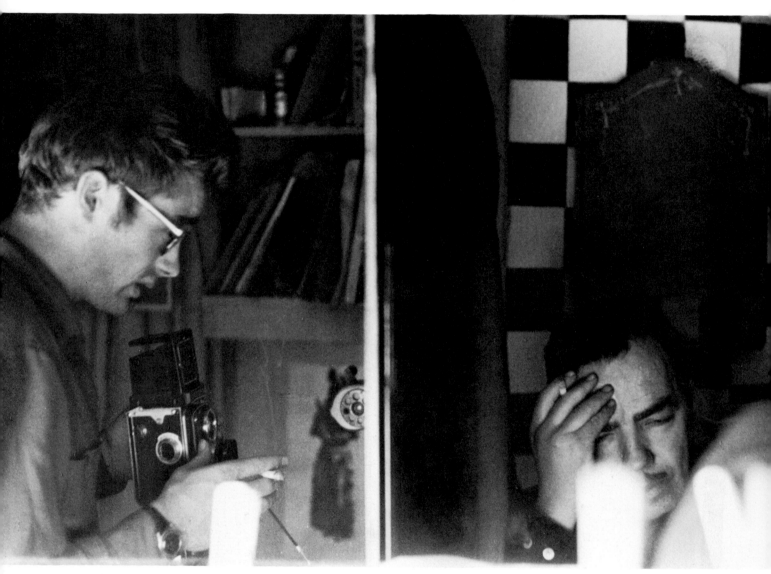

*Bob Heller*

Jimmy setting up an illustrative shot of me. Dean's shot of me
captures a sick villain quality.

*James Dean*

When Dean became famous, he set out to change his image
by chopping his hair short.

A crowd of us, here consisting of Marty Landau, Billy Gunn,
Bob Heller, Israel Citkowitz, Lenny Rosenman and others,
often met on the roof of the Museum of Modern Art (*following
pages*).

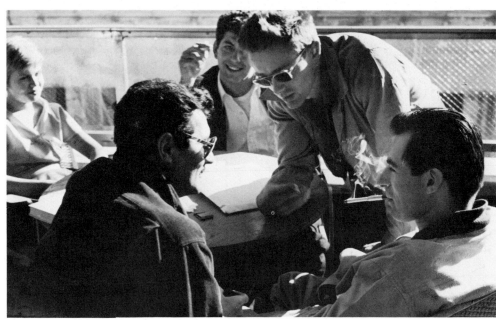

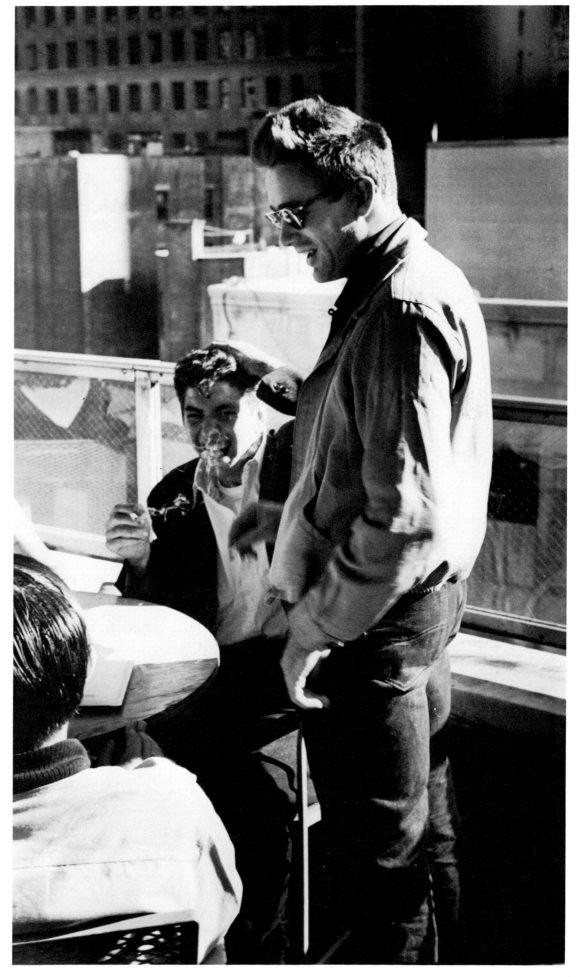

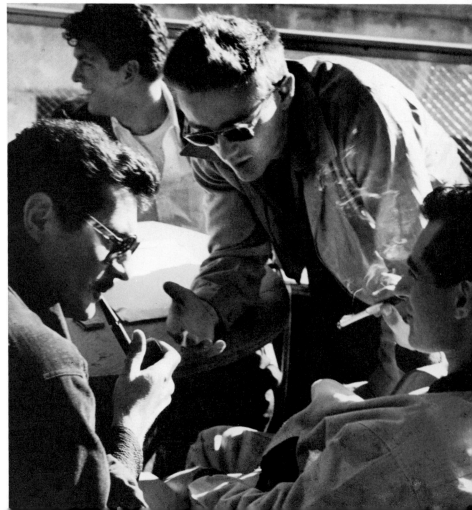

*James Dean*

*James Dean*

James Dean shot of Bob Heller.

Dean preparing for a role he wanted in "Bus Stop," including biting the tips of his fingers to sensitize them as a gunfighter would (*opposite*).

Jimmy and Marty at Riker's on 57th Street.

Bob Heller and Jimmy at the counter in Cromwell's Pharmacy.

Dean in his self-made movie phase reading the
light at the fountainhead in my garden.

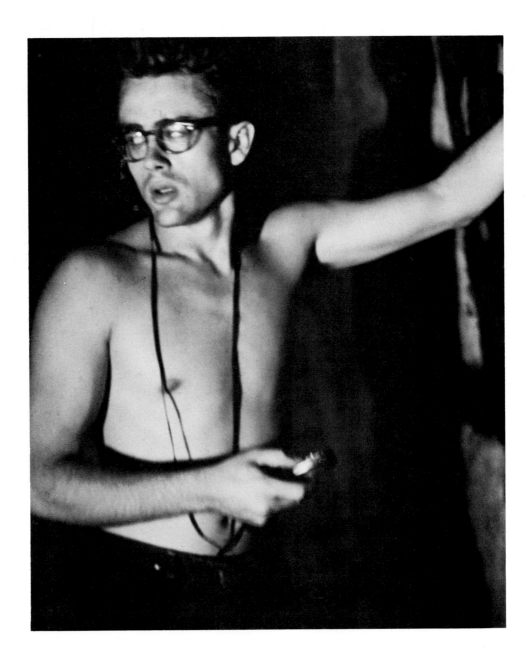

New Year's Eve party at my place. From left: Barbara Glenn,
Billy Gunn, Jim, Marty Landau, Bob Heller and Tony Ray, son
of Nick Ray, director of *Rebel Without a Cause*.

"I'm playing the damn bongo and the world go to hell," Jimmy would say.

Rehearsal at the Cherry Lane Theater for *Women of Trachis*
for the New School for Social Research, February 12, 1954.
James Dean with Eli Wallach.

Barbara Baxley and James Dean assisting my shooting of
Lenny Rosenman. The occasion was a birthday party at Jo Van
Fleet's for Rosenman, who wrote the music for *East of Eden,*
and a number of the cast members were there. Jimmy had fun
shooting Jo Van Fleet (*following pages*).

*James Dean*

*James Dean*

*James Dean*

The James Dean/Mary Astor "affair" between takes of the TV rehearsal for "The Thief."

Jimmy aiming through Mary Astor's earring on Second
Avenue, followed by "wearing" a chandelier.

Dean didn't always stick to the script during rehearsals.

Lunching and rehearsing with the
cast of "The Thief": Mary Astor,
Diana Lynn and Patrick Knowles.

Jim mugging to Roy, with Diana Lynn following right along,
during a take of "The Thief."

"Look, Roy, Picasso!"

On the set of "The Thief."

Dean backstage in his dressing room.

Relaxing near the set (*following pages*).

"Hey, Roy, you hold the camera and I'll press the button."

Jim liked sometimes to be off by himself . . . thinking,
dreaming—I don't know what (*following pages*).

Jim liked jazz and listened wherever he found it.

# Epilogue

It has been my intention, through the text and pictures presented here, to show the whole James Dean as I knew him. He affected those who knew him and a great many who didn't. We still remember him, but in the 26 years since he died the world has changed, and he would have changed with it. If only we were 26 years younger—but we're not.

*Bob Heller*

"I told you I couldn't be hypnotized," the result of an attempt by a medium to contact Dean "in the beyond."

*Bob Heller*